ESEA
TITLE I

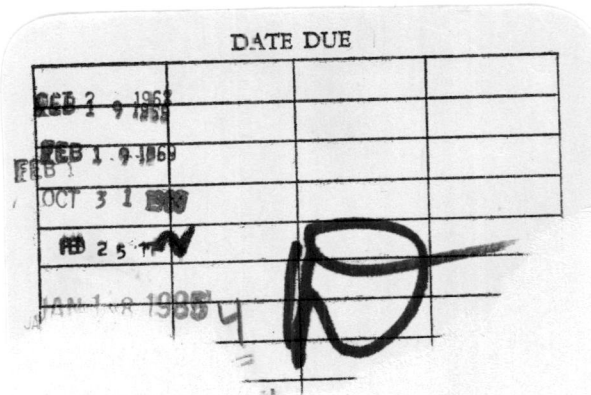

Pajaro Valley Unified School District
HALL DISTRICT SCHOOL

The Discovery Books are prepared under the educational supervision of

Mary C. Austin, Ed.D.

Reading Specialist

and Lecturer on Education

Harvard University

A DISCOVERY BOOK

by Lillie Patterson

illustrated by Anthony D'Adamo

GARRARD PUBLISHING COMPANY
CHAMPAIGN, ILLINOIS

Booker T. Washington
Leader of His People

Pajaro Valley Unified School District
HALL DISTRICT SCHOOL

This book is for
> My father, Alex Patterson
> and
> My physician, Dr. Ralph Young
> Both leaders of their people.

Copyright 1962 by Lillie Patterson
Manufactured in the United States of America
Library of Congress Catalog Number: 62-7331

Contents

Booker T. Washington: Leader of His People

CHAPTER		Page
1	A Slave Boy Called Booker	7
2	Songs of Freedom	13
3	A New Home	19
4	New Names—New Hope	25
5	The Student	31
6	Teacher and Indian Chief	39
7	The New School	45
8	First Things First	53
9	"Mr. B. T."	61
10	A Famous Speech	67
11	A New Day for the Negroes	73

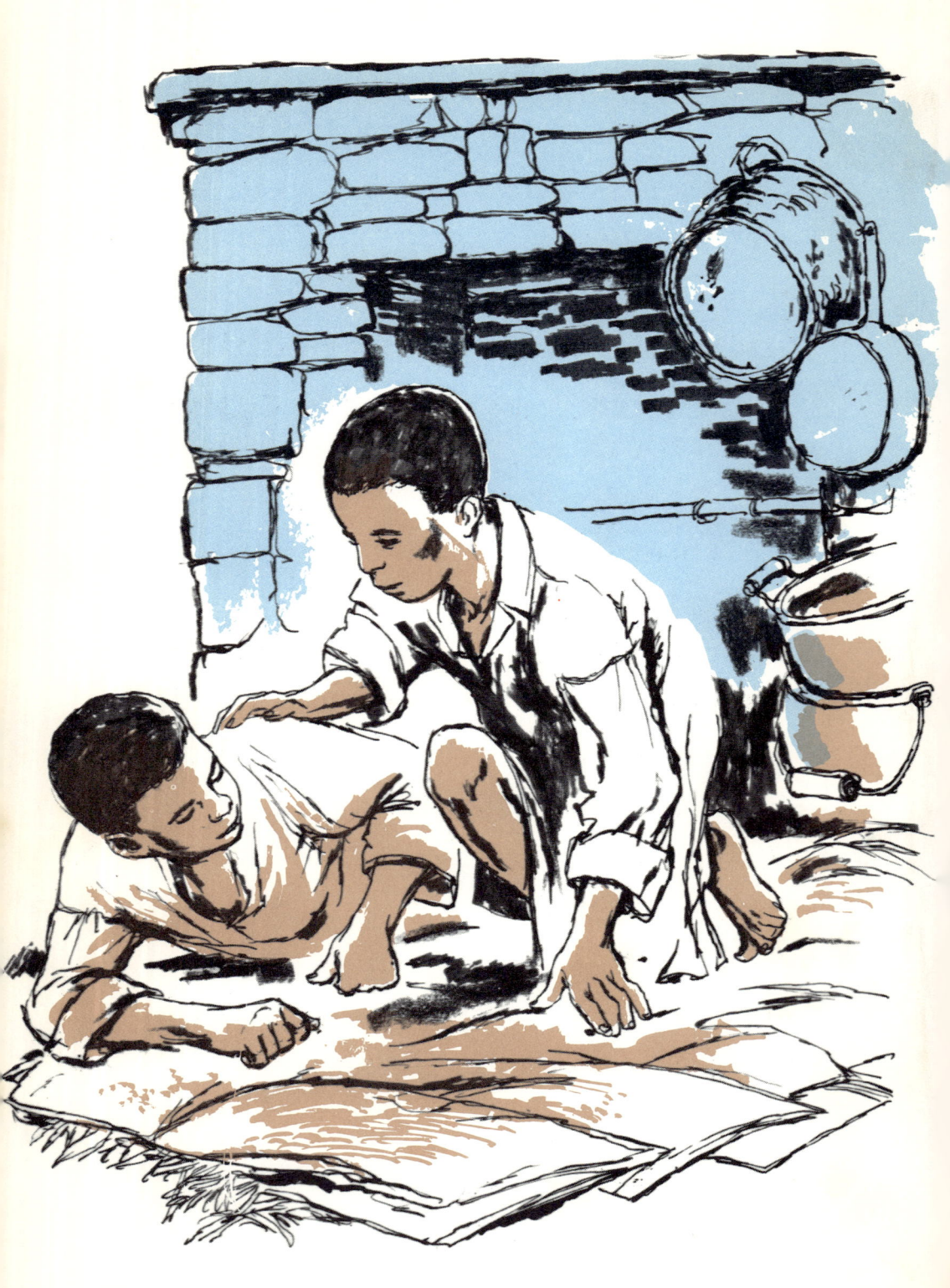

Chapter 1

A Slave Boy Called Booker

The summer sun woke Booker. It streamed into the one-room slave cabin.

Seven-year-old Booker blinked sleep from his eyes. Then he shook his sleeping brother. "Wake up, John! Sun's high!" The boys slept on the floor on a pallet made of grain sacks. Baby sister Amanda, called Mandy, slept on another pallet.

There was almost no furniture in the cabin. The floor was the bare earth. A rough wooden table stood against one wall. Two benches were also in the room. But there was no real bed, no stove. Beside a big stone fireplace hung iron pots and kettles. Booker's mother was the plantation cook. Plantations are big farms or estates.

The door opened. Booker jumped across the potato hole in the middle of the floor. Sweet potatoes were stored in the hole in winter months. "Good morning, Ma!" Booker called.

"Good morning, son." Booker's mother kissed his light brown face, his wide forehead. "You're growing like a weed."

Her name was Jane. Most slaves had only one name.

"Did you bring our Sunday treat, Ma?"

"Two treats!" Jane reached into a basket. "Here's the first one."

"No! No!" Booker backed away, his eyes wide with horror. "Not a new shirt, Ma."

"I know it's rough, Booker. But in a few weeks it will be as soft as one made of cotton."

They lived in Franklin County, Virginia. There, slave clothes were made from flax. Slave boys wore a shirt that came down to their knees. Sharp bits of flax pricked like needles.

"My poor skin!" Booker moaned.

Eleven-year-old John walked over to his mother. "I'll wear the shirt until it's soft," he said.

The Sunday treat was molasses. Other times they ate only corn bread and fat pork. Booker tipped his tin plate until the sweet molasses ran all over it. "This always makes it seem more," he said.

Booker's owner was James Burroughs. It was 1863. The Civil War was being fought between the North and the South. Abraham Lincoln was President.

Booker helped Mrs. Burroughs in the house and yards. One day she said, "You must walk with my daughters to school and carry their books."

"Yes, ma'am." Booker was always happy out of doors.

They reached the school. Booker peeked into the sunny room. The boys and girls were reading.

"Going to school must be heaven," the slave boy whispered.

That night he said, "I want to learn to read, Ma."

"I know, Booker. Every night I pray for freedom. I hope your Pa is free now." Jane's husband, Washington Ferguson, was stepfather to Booker and John. He had run away from his owner.

"Why can't slaves go to school?" Booker asked.

"Hush! It's against the law. You keep hoping, child. I'll keep praying."

"I will, Ma. And when I learn, I'll teach all the slaves in the world to read."

Chapter 2

Songs of Freedom

Months passed. The Civil War went on. The Burroughs family became poorer and poorer.

Booker had to do more and more of the work. He did it gladly. The slaves felt sorry for their owners. Each week now Booker took the corn to the mill to be ground. He enjoyed listening to the slaves he met there. They always shared the latest news.

Not a one of the slaves could read. Yet they often knew of many happenings long before their owners. Secrets were passed from kitchen to kitchen, from field to field. Slaves called their news system the "grapevine telegraph."

Each day after 1864 news became more exciting. The grapevine telegraph buzzed night and day. "Mr. Lincoln's army is winning! The war will soon be over! All slaves will be free!"

Slaves couldn't stop singing. They made up songs about the day of "jubilo." That was the joyful day they would be free. *"Freedom was in the air, and had been for many months,"* Booker remembered later.

One spring day in 1865, Mrs. Burroughs sent for her slaves.

They came running. The Burroughs family stood on the porch of their home. All of them were crying.

A man in uniform stepped forward. He read a long paper to the slaves. "This is the Emancipation Proclamation," he explained. "It says that you are free. The war is over. Slavery is ended in the United States."

"Free at last!" A joyful shout rang over the plantation.

Some slaves began to sing. Others started to pray.

Jane dropped to her knees. Tears ran down her cheeks. She gathered Booker, John and Mandy in her arms. Then she looked up into the bright blue sky. "Thank you, Lord. My prayers are answered."

The freed slaves wandered about like lost children. They had no food, no homes, no jobs. What would become of them?

Booker's family was lucky. One morning John called, "Booker! Look what's in front of our cabin!"

"A donkey!" Booker cried.

A soldier had brought the donkey, a cart, and some wonderful news. Booker's stepfather had followed Northern soldiers to West Virginia. Now he wanted his family to come to the town of Malden.

Mrs. Burroughs gave them some food and pots and pans. "Please send word back to me," she said. Jane and Mrs. Burroughs were both crying.

"I'll write," Booker promised. "I'll write as soon as I go to school."

"Good-by!"

"Good-by!"

Jane and Mandy rode in the cart. Booker and John walked behind, kicking the dirt happily with their bare feet. None of them had ever been away from Franklin County. None of them could read a word. Yet they bravely set out on a two-hundred-mile trip.

For it was 1865, the magical year of jubilo.

Chapter 3

A New Home

The trip took many weeks. The family went mile after mile over mountains. Kind strangers helped them to find the right roads. They cooked their meals over campfires. At night they slept under the stars.

Finally they reached Malden. How happy Ferguson was to see them! "The cabin is not much," he said. "But it's our home."

He was right. The cabin was no better than the one they left behind. "I'll fix it up," John promised. "I'll try to build a kitchen and some tables and benches."

Booker's eyes gleamed with excitement. "Where is the school, Pa? Can I start tomorrow?"

"School?" Ferguson frowned. "There's no school here. Besides, you boys must start to work tomorrow."

Booker's high hopes fell. He was too disappointed to say another word.

Jane asked, "Where will they work? Booker is only nine."

"They will work in the salt mines!"

Booker shivered at the sound of the words. He had been so sure that freedom would mean learning to read.

The salt mines were wells dug deep into the earth. Salt water was pumped up from them. When the water was boiled away, wet salt was left. The salt was then dried. Both Booker and John became packers. They beat the salt down into big barrels. The work was hard, even for grown men.

One day as Booker walked home he saw an amazing sight. A strange Negro sat on a barrel. Other Negroes stood around, listening. The stranger was reading a newspaper to them.

"He is reading!" Booker cried. "He is a Negro and he's reading! If he can do it, so will I."

But there was nothing for Booker to read. There was not even a torn page from a magazine to be found.

Then Booker saw that each salt barrel was marked with a number. He began to read by learning these numbers.

One evening his mother said, "I have a big surprise for you." She gave him a gift.

"A book!" Booker held it gently.

"It's a Webster's Blue-Backed Speller," Jane said. "I saved a little each week to buy it."

Each night after that Booker went to sleep over his book. He studied it very hard until he learned the alphabet. Soon he could read a few words.

Then an exciting thing happened. A school opened in Malden. Booker was overjoyed. "Please let me go," he begged his stepfather.

Ferguson explained, "We are poor.

We get very little money for our work. Everyone must work if we are to eat."

Booker's chin trembled. But he was stubborn. "I *am* going to school," he told himself. Each day he begged. So did his mother.

At last Ferguson said, "You can go. But you will have to work before and after school."

"Oh, I will!" Booker promised. "I'll do anything to go to school."

Booker's real day of jubilo had come.

Chapter 4

New Names—
New Hope

It was Booker's first day in school. "What is your name?" the teacher asked.

"Booker, sir."

"Booker, *what?*"

"Oh, dear!" Booker thought. "I need a last name. Which shall I choose?" Then he remembered one very famous name.

"*Washington!*" he answered. "Booker Washington, sir."

That day went well. So did all the days during the next months. He was always up before daylight. There was a two-mile walk to work. He packed salt, then ran to school, then hurried back to work. This was Booker's day.

But he was a happy schoolboy with a fine new name. He had a new brother, too. Jane adopted an orphan boy named James. John, Mandy and James all added Booker's last name to their own.

Booker did not go to school long. His stepfather made him leave school to work in the coal mines.

How Booker hated the work under the ground! He still dreamed about going to school. One day he heard two miners talking about a new school.

"Are you sure it's for colored boys?" the first asked.

"That's right," the other answered. "It's for poor colored students."

"And what's the name of this school?"

Booker thought he would burst with excitement as he waited. Then the answer came over the coal dust.

"Hampton!"

"I'm going to that school," Booker promised himself. "I don't know how I'll get there. But I'm going."

Not long after that, Booker got another job. Mrs. Ruffner was the wife of the owner of the mines. She needed help. Booker knew that she was hard to please.

Mrs. Ruffner promised, "If you please me I will lend you my books."

Booker did please her. Mrs. Ruffner taught him how to take pride in his work. And she let him go to school part of the time.

When Booker was sixteen, he decided to go to find Hampton. He bought a cheap bag to carry his things. His mother and John saved a little money to buy him some clothes.

Before Booker left home his mother told him something special. She had named him Booker Taliaferro when he was born. So his name became Booker Taliaferro Washington.

Booker started out by horse-drawn stagecoach. Later he took the train. When his money gave out, he started to walk. Finally he reached Richmond, Virginia. Now what would he do next?

After a while, he found a high wooden sidewalk and went to sleep under it. The next day he got a job loading iron onto a ship. Each night he slept outdoors so he could save money for his trip.

Autumn was Booker's favorite season. It was autumn when he reached Hampton. How beautiful the campus looked! A campus is the grounds of a college. Trees were bright with red and orange and yellow. Among them stood a tall brick building. Boats sailed upon the blue water nearby.

Later Booker said, *"I felt that I had reached the promised land."*

Chapter 5

The Student

"I am Miss Mary Mackie, the head teacher."

Booker faced the white teacher. He was ragged and dirty from his long trip. "Please!" he begged. "Please let me stay here and go to school."

Miss Mackie only said, "The next room needs sweeping. Take the broom and sweep it."

This was his test. "How glad I am that I worked for Mrs. Ruffner!" Booker thought.

Booker gladly swept the whole room once, twice, three times. Then he dusted everything in it four times. He washed the woodwork. He shined the doorknobs.

Miss Mackie returned. She rubbed a snowy white handkerchief over tables and benches. Booker held his breath. But not a speck of dust was anywhere. Miss Mackie smiled and said, "I guess you will do to enter this school."

Booker's heart leaped with joy. "I'll make good," he promised.

Miss Mackie gave Booker a job as school janitor. He made the fires each morning before school. He cleaned the rooms each afternoon. No work was too hard. John sent a few dollars whenever he could.

Booker liked all of his teachers.

Hampton teachers were from rich white families. They were spending their lives teaching Negroes.

Best of all Booker liked the principal, Samuel Chapman Armstrong. Armstrong was tall and handsome with flashing eyes. He had joined the Northern Army during the Civil War. He was then a young man just out of college. He became interested in the Negroes. *"I see only the four million slaves, and for them I fight."*

After the war General Armstrong said, "The freed slaves need schools." His friends helped him buy a plantation in Hampton, Virginia. In 1868 he opened Hampton Institute there. The school trained teachers. It also taught useful trades, such as carpentry.

"The General is wonderful!" Booker said. "I am going to be like him."

Miss Nathalie Lord taught Booker reading. One day she told him, "You have a fine voice. You could become a great speaker. I will use my spare hours to teach you." She taught Booker how to stand and how to breathe. She showed him how to use his hands and his body when he spoke.

Booker was very shy at first.

"Hold a pencil in your hand," Miss Lord said.

This worked. After that, Booker always held a pencil when he gave a speech.

Two years passed. Booker went home for the summer. His family had saved the money to send for him. How happy Jane was to see her son again!

But a sad thing happened. Jane died soon after Booker got home. Booker was shocked. "I wanted to do so much for Ma," he told John.

"You can finish school," John said. "That's what she wanted."

"I will!" Booker promised. "And I will send you and James and Mandy to Hampton. Then Ma's wish will really come true."

Booker finished Hampton in 1875. General Armstrong said, *"Help your people by giving them what has been given to you."*

Chapter 6

Teacher and Indian Chief

Booker went back home to teach in Malden. He was now called Professor Washington.

His day began at eight o'clock. He taught more than eighty students in day school. Then he worked on until ten at night, for he had opened a night school. He taught two Sunday schools too. *"I taught anyone who wanted to learn anything that I could teach him,"* Washington said later.

He also gave special lessons to students who wanted to go to Hampton. John got very special teaching. Soon Booker sent his faithful brother to Hampton.

After three years Washington went to school again. He studied in Washington, D. C., the nation's capital.

"You should study law," some friends said.

"You should go into politics," said others.

Washington began to study law. But he soon forgot both law and politics, for an exciting letter came from General Armstrong.

"I need you," he wrote. "We are beginning an experiment for the United States Government. I want to prove that Indians, too, can be educated."

At that time most people said that Indians were too wild to be taught.

Washington returned to Hampton. "I will put the Indians in your care," General Armstrong said. "If we can teach the Indians, then the Government might build schools for them."

Soon nearly a hundred young Indians arrived from the West. Washington smiled and said, "Greetings!"

Loud grunts came from the Indians. They could not speak a word of English. Their eyes were angry. They did not want to change their ways of living.

Washington knew how the Indians felt. They are a proud people. Now they would have to give up many old customs. They would have to dress as other students.

"Oh, my!" Washington thought. "How can I make friends with them?"

He found the answer. He used his big smile and his friendly handshake. He was kind and understanding. "There are many ways of showing brotherhood," he said.

Washington told the students, "We can learn from the Indians." There was one custom the whole school liked. Indians wore soft moccasins on their feet. Soon everyone on the campus gave up shoes for the comfortable moccasins.

The Indians lived in a new building. The students named it the *"Wigwam."* Washington lived with them as their *"housefather."* Everyone called him *"Chief."* As he taught the Indians to speak English, he won their friendship.

Soon he began teaching them other things. Before the end of that year the Indians looked to Washington as their leader. "You are really our Chief," they said.

The experiment was a big success. The President and Congress praised it. Hundreds of Indians came to Hampton to study. Later the Government opened a special school for Indians.

Washington had done a great thing for the Indians, and for America.

"And I learned, too," Washington said. "I must not think only of helping the Negroes. I must try to help all people."

Chapter 7

The New School

Now came the biggest surprise of all.

One evening in May, 1881, General Armstrong read a letter to his students. It came from Tuskegee, Alabama, a small town in the deep South.

The letter was from a group of Tuskegee men. One was a white banker, who had once owned slaves. Another was a Negro shoemaker, who had once been a slave. "Our state has given money to start a school for Negroes," they said. "Please send one of your teachers to be principal."

The next day Armstrong sent for Washington. "I believe you are the person to send. Will you go?"

"I am very willing to try, General Armstrong."

They wrote to Tuskegee. The answer came, *"Booker T. Washington will suit us. Send him at once."*

What an honor for a young man only twenty-five years old!

Washington arrived in Tuskegee that June. The town had been named for an Indian chief. Washington could not guess that he, a Negro, would make it famous.

"Where's the schoolhouse?" he asked.

There was no schoolhouse. There were no students. "How can I start a school with nothing?" Washington wondered.

But he did not give up. "I will visit Negro families," he said. "Then I will know the kind of school they need."

Washington traveled the dusty roads to tell the people about the new school. He slept in the tumbledown cabins. He ate the corn bread and pork which was still the main food. How poor the Negroes were! They planted nothing but cotton. They had to share their cotton with their white landlords.

"My people are free," Washington said sadly. "But they have to be taught how to live in freedom."

Where could he begin? Washington formed his idea of education. *"Leadership consists in finding folk where they are and guiding them to where they ought to be."*

He said, "Negroes need more than book learning just now. I will teach them better ways of farming and useful trades. Then they can earn more money. I will show them how to plant vegetables and eat healthier meals. I will help them save money to buy land and build homes. Then their everyday lives will be happier."

Washington borrowed an old church building. And on the Fourth of July, 1881, he opened his school. There were thirty students. Many were grown men and women.

The school became known as Tuskegee Normal and Industrial Institute. Normal meant that it trained teachers. Industrial meant that it taught useful trades, or industries.

The beginning was not easy. There were few books and almost no furniture. When it rained the water came through holes in the roof. Students would run to hold an umbrella over their teacher.

"Nothing will stop our school from growing," Washington told his students. "We will use what we have and work to get more."

New students came, begging to stay. Washington could never send them away. "I always think of the day I stood before Miss Mackie at Hampton," he said.

He hired another teacher, Olivia Davidson, who was fair and pretty. She became Lady Principal. She worked as hard as Washington. Olivia, too, wanted to spend her life helping her people.

Chapter 8

First Things First

An old plantation came up for sale. Washington borrowed some money from Hampton and bought it. The plantation had two cabins, a stable, and a henhouse. Washington and his students cleaned and painted. Then the school moved. The stable and henhouse became classrooms.

Meanwhile the Lady Principal was busy raising money to pay back the loan. The whole town helped. Some could give only a few pennies. Others came to work.

One day an old, old woman came. "I spent most of my life in slavery," she said. "I have saved six eggs. Please let these eggs help the new school."

"Thank you," Washington said. "No gift will ever mean more to me."

Washington told his students, "Bring your axes to school tomorrow. We will have our first Chopping Bee."

"We've never been to a Chopping Bee," students cried excitedly.

Washington led them into the woods. "Follow me!" he said. He began chopping trees.

The students followed. Suddenly one cried, "Hey! This is nothing but cutting trees and clearing land."

"*First things first!*" Washington explained. "First we will clear land.

Then we will plant a farm so that we can eat."

Students grumbled, "We came here to school for book learning."

"Book learning? Why, of course!" Washington said. "But hand work and head work must go together. A good carpenter must know arithmetic. A good farmer must know science."

"But we want to be teachers," the students said.

"And you must teach Negroes that there is beauty and dignity in working with the hands." Washington said, *"There is as much dignity in tilling a field as in writing a poem."*

Summer came. Washington went to Malden to get married. His bride was his childhood sweetheart, Fannie Smith.

She, too, had gone to Hampton. Fannie had beautiful eyes and a merry laugh.

"Next things next!" Washington said. "We must have more buildings. Our students must live on the campus. We must teach them to keep healthy and clean."

The first building was made of wood. "Our next will be of bricks," Washington told the students.

"Bricks?" students said. "There are no brickyards nearby."

"We will make our own bricks. There is good clay here."

"But have you ever made bricks, Mr. Washington?"

"We learn by doing!"

Students dug the clay and shaped 25,000 bricks. It was a hard job.

Washington made a special oven, or kiln to bake them. But the kiln did not work right. The bricks crumbled. A second kiln failed. So did a third.

Washington sold his watch in town to get money for another kiln. Again bricks were shaped and baked. Everyone waited. When the kiln was opened, a shout went up. "Bricks! Perfect ones!"

Men from town came to buy bricks. They said, "We will help the school, because the school is helping the town."

"Yes," Washington said. "The town and school will each help the other."

That year a baby girl was born to Washington and Fannie. They named her Portia. A few months later Fannie died. Washington cared for baby Portia and worked harder than ever.

Then General Armstrong came to visit. The two men spent long hours talking and planning. "We must help the whole South," Armstrong said.

"Ah, yes!" Washington promised. "I forgive the Southern white man for keeping the Negroes as slaves. *I will let no man drag me down so low as to make me hate him.*"

Chapter 9

"Mr. B. T."

The school grew rapidly. New buildings went up! More land was bought! New teachers came!

"Where will I get money for such a growing school?" Washington wondered.

General Armstrong gave the answer. He taught Washington how to make speeches to raise money.

Washington traveled all over the United States. He told people about the school. They sent money to Tuskegee.

They sent clothes and blankets for the poor students. "Washington can talk people into doing just what he wants them to do," many said.

By 1885 things brightened. John came. "Booker needs me," John said. He gave up his own work. He spent the rest of his life helping his brother to build Tuskegee. Later James, too, came to help.

And Washington married Olivia Davidson, the Lady Principal. Soon there were two little boys in the family, Booker Taliaferro, and Ernest Davidson.

One cold winter night their house caught on fire. The babies were saved. But Olivia caught a terrible cold and soon died. Washington was so sad! He was very good to his three children.

He told them wonderful stories at bedtime. He took them for walks in the woods. They picked flowers and listened to bird songs. "Always stay close to nature," Washington taught.

When Washington went on trips, he bought gifts for John's children as well as for his own. Often he took one of the children with him. He took John's little girl all the way to California.

Small Portia loved music. How she loved to play the piano for her father! Washington was very proud of his little daughter.

Often, before Washington gave a speech, he said it to Portia. "How do you like it?" he would ask.

"Oh, Father, it's grand!" Portia would reply.

And Washington was like a father to his students. He knew each by name. They lovingly called him *"Mr. B. T."* Each year students went out to teach others what they had learned. Many opened schools of their own.

Washington told students, "We train your hand, head and heart. *And we help you in these ways that you, in turn, may help others.*"

He was too busy to take vacations. But he had his own garden. He raised chickens and pigs. He gathered eggs and vegetables for the family. "I rest when I am close to the soil," he said.

And Washington loved horses. A rich white friend gave him a swift gray horse, Dexter. "No horse will ever run fast enough for you," the friend said.

After a hard day's work Washington would mount Dexter and gallop over the countryside. Sometimes he would stop suddenly, very still, to hear a bird or a cricket singing.

Step by step, Washington made the school larger. The students who came often had no money. So they built the buildings themselves. They grew the food they ate. They made the things they needed. And they learned useful trades as they worked. "We are doing more than building a school," Washington said. "We are lifting a race."

A stranger came to visit Tuskegee. Later someone asked him, "Did you see Washington's school?"

"*School!*" the stranger cried. "*I have seen Booker T. Washington's city.*"

Chapter 10

A Famous Speech

It was September, 1895. Atlanta, capital city of Georgia, buzzed with excitement. A big fair was about to open there. It would show the many uses of cotton. It would also show things the South had done since the Civil War.

Newspapers carried surprising news. Booker T. Washington would give one of the opening speeches. A Negro had never spoken at such an event in the South!

"What will he say?" people asked. "Will he say the South is unfair to Negroes? Will he spoil the fun of the fair?"

"What can I say?" Washington asked himself. "Negroes, Northerners and Southerners, will all be listening. My own future, and that of my school and my race, will depend upon what I say."

Yes, visitors were there from every state and from other lands. Cannons boomed! Whistles tooted! Bands played! Parades marched! Atlanta was like a big circus tent.

The opening speeches began. The hall was packed. The Governor, the Mayor and other famous people spoke.

Then Washington's turn came. He rose, holding a pencil in his hand.

He stood tall and straight as an Indian chief. He turned his handsome head toward the sun. His voice rang out.

Washington begged all the people to work together to build up the South. He told Negroes to stay in the South and to make friends with their white neighbors. He told them to get training, to do their work better and to help the South grow.

He told white listeners to give Negroes a chance to learn. Negroes had been faithful workers. The two races could help each other, and the South.

Then Washington raised his hand. He told the people to obey the law and to work together. *"This will bring into our beloved South a new heaven and a new earth."*

White and colored stood and cheered as one. Men tossed their hats into the air! Women waved their handkerchiefs! It was as though everyone had been put under a magic spell by the words of Booker T. Washington.

Newspapers said, "It was one of the greatest speeches ever given in the South."

And Washington became famous overnight! He was now the leader of the Negro race. Harvard University gave him an honorary degree. It was the first time a great American school had given a degree of honor to a Negro. The President of Harvard said, *"Booker Taliaferro Washington — teacher; wise helper of his race; good servant of God and country."*

Washington gave other great speeches. Halls were packed wherever he spoke. He would speak to a group of college presidents and teachers. Then he would leave and talk to a group of poor Negroes. He knew just what to say to every group. He loved to tell funny stories. He could make his listeners laugh one minute and cry the next.

In 1899, friends gave Washington money for a trip to Europe. He was now married to Margaret Murray, one of the teachers at Tuskegee. They were entertained by the most important people in Europe. They had tea with Queen Victoria in her castle. The boy born in a slave cabin was guest of the Queen of England.

Chapter 11

A New Day for the Negroes

The next year Washington wrote the story of his life. *Up from Slavery* became a best seller. The whole world read it. Later Washington wrote other books about his work and his race.

And like magic, he brought just the right teachers to work at the school. One teacher said, *"It was teamwork that built Tuskegee."*

The most famous teacher was George Washington Carver. He came to teach agricultural science. The gentle Negro scientist and Washington became close friends. Late at night the two walked peacefully over the campus. They planned help for the farmers.

"We'll show them how to make the soil richer," Carver said.

"And we'll teach them to keep pigs and cows," Washington added.

"They'll plant sweet potatoes, peanuts and soybeans, along with cotton. Then the South will grow richer."

"And they'll have better schools," Washington said. "Then the South will grow wiser."

Carver's work brought world-wide fame to Tuskegee.

Washington's fame spread, too. He received more than 150 letters a day! Kings and statesmen asked his advice. President Theodore Roosevelt invited him to the White House for dinner. Dartmouth College gave him another degree of honor. Now he was called Dr. Washington.

Years passed. Soon it was 1906. "I can't believe that the school is twenty-five years old," Washington said. "And I am fifty." What a grand celebration the school had that year!

In 1907 Portia married. Portia had studied music in Europe. She, too, gave help to Tuskegee. She trained the singers in the famous Tuskegee Choir.

Washington worked harder than ever. Sometimes he gave six speeches in a day.

He often had to be away from Tuskegee. But daily letters told him just what was happening there. He even knew how many eggs the chickens laid, and what the students ate for dinner.

On his travels, Washington made friends with some of the richest men in America.

Julius Rosenwald was head of Sears, Roebuck and Company. Washington asked him, "Will you help the Negroes build schools?"

Rosenwald gave money for more than five thousand Negro schools throughout the South.

Washington asked another friend, Miss Anna Jeanes, "Will you help us train teachers?"

Miss Jeanes gave a million dollars.

Andrew Carnegie, another famous American, helped. He said, *"History is to know two Washingtons, one white, the other black, both Fathers of their people."*

1915 was a busy year. Washington became tired. He was asked to speak at a big meeting in the North. Before he left, he went to see Carver. The two men looked over the beautiful campus.

"Tuskegee has come a long way," Washington said.

Carver smiled gently. "So have we. You and I were both born slaves. Yet, we are helping to build a great school."

"My school and my race," Washington said, "have both made progress. Now we look to the future. A new day for the Negroes lies ahead."

Washington went north. There, he became very sick. *"Take me home,"* he said. *"I was born in the South, I have lived and labored in the South, and I wish to die and be buried in the South."*

He reached Tuskegee. Early the next morning he died peacefully. It was harvest time, his favorite season.

Washington gave many gifts to his country. Perhaps his greatest gift was the lesson he taught, *All men are brothers.*

Even today his name has magic. A Southern farmer will say on a lovely morning, "It's going to be a wonderful day!"

"Ah, yes!" his wife will reply. "It's going to be a real Booker T. Washington Day."